To Bill Seiler
+ Family —
Best regards,
Philip Blackburn
Aug. 10, 1990

EVERY, EVERY DAY

(FOR THOSE WHO LOVE)

BY PHILIP BLACKBURN
ILLUSTRATED BY JOLENE BROWN

Printed by Cody Publications, Inc.
Kissimmee, Florida

To
Rod McKuen
Poet, Composer, Writer, Singer

You have made this world
  a better place by your
  words and by your music.
I salute your extraordinary
  talents.
I thank you for your encouragement.

PHB
a june midnight, 1984.

HOW MUCH DO YOU LOVE ME ?

I REALLY LIKE TO HEAR

THE WAY YOUR WORD

EACH OUT FOR ME,

WHEN YOU TELL ME I AM DEAR.

DO YOU LOVE ME AS A RAINBOW

DO YOU LOVE ME, LOVE ME, LOVE ME ?

LOVES HER COLOR BLUE?

PLEASE TELL ME THAT YOU DO.

DO YOU LOVE ME
IN THE SAME WAY
THAT THE MOON
LOVES THE SUN?

AND AS DEEPLY AS
THE EVENING STARS
LOVE THEIR NIGHTTIME FUN?

DO YOU LOVE ME AS THE OCEA

DO YOU LOVE M

OVES ITS GENTLE SPRAY ?

OVE ME, LOVE ME

EVERY, EVERY DAY ?

to someone special

THERE ARE TIMES I NEED
          TO HEAR YOUR LOVE
AND FEEL AND SEE IT, TOO.

BUT I ALWAYS NEED
          TO KNOW YOUR LOVE
FOR NOTHING ELSE WILL DO.

DO YOU LOVE ME AS THE HEATHE

IF YOU .... LOVE M

THEN TELL M

OVES THE MORNING DEW?

T LEAST THAT MUCH,

HAT YOU DO.

AND DO YOU KNOW HOW SNOWFLAKES
LOVE THE MOUNTAIN AIR ?

IS THE LOVE YOU HAVE FOR ME

LIKE THAT ?

IS IT ALWAYS THERE ?

YOU HAVE SMELLED THE WAY

THE RAIN IS LOVED

BY THE FLOWERS AND THE TREES

WILL YOU TELL ME

I AM LOVED LIKE THAT ?

TELL ME _ WILL YOU PLEASE ?

WILL YOU LOVE ME ON THE COLD DAY

WILL YOU KNOW THE TIMES

I NEED TO HEAR

HOW MUCH I MEAN TO YOU ?

AND WHEN I'M FEELING LONELY

AND

THE

DAY'S

BEEN

LONG

AND

BAD

WILL YOU HUG AND KISS AND HOLD ME
AND LOVE AWAY THE SAD?

I LOVE YOU, LOVE YOU, LOVE YOU
EVERY, EVERY DAY.

I LOVE YOU WHEN YOU'RE WITH ME
I LOVE YOU WHEN YOU'RE AWAY.

I LOVE YOU BECAUSE
YOU'RE SPECIAL
IN YOUR GENTLE LOVING WAY.

I LOVE YOU, LOVE YOU,
LOVE YOU
EVERY, EVERY DAY.

I LOVE YOU LOTS ON SUNDAYS

MONDAYS AND TUESDAYS, TO

WEDNESDAY.

THURSDAYS AND FRIDAYS

SATURDAYS, I DO.

I LOVE YOU MOST IN SPECIAL MONTH

I LOVE YOU, LOV

EVERY

HE MONTHS FROM JUNE THROUGH MAY

'OU, LOVE YOU

:VERY DAY.

SOMETIMES MY LOVE IS QUIE

SOMETIMES MY LOVE IS NOIS

KE THE FOREST IN THE NIGHT.

S I SHOUT WITH ALL MY MIGHT.

SOMETIMES MY LOVE IS TENDE

SOMETIMES MY LOVE IS FORCEFU

IKE A BABY'S SWEET EMBRACE,

OU CAN SEE IT IN MY FACE.

AND WHEN THE WORLD

HAS HURT YOU

AND UNCARING WINDS

HAVE BLOWN,

MY LOVE WILL TOUCH

AND HOLD YOU

SO YOU'LL NEVER BE ALONE.

AND WHEN YOU'RE FEELING LONELY

AND EVERYTHING SEEMS BAD,

I'LL LOVE YOU 'TIL YOU'RE HAPPY.

I'LL LOVE AWAY THE SAD.

MY LOVE IS ALWAYS WITH YO

WITH ITS WAR

ND TENDER GLOW.

MY LOVE

SURROUNDS

AND FOLLOWS YOU

WHEREVER YOU MAY GO.

I LOVE YOU WITH THE GLADNES

F A PUPPY'S GIVING HEART

AND THOUGH I LOVE YOU
ALL THESE WAYS
I'VE ONLY MADE A START

FOR ALL OF THE TOMORROWS
AND FOR ALWAYS AND A DAY,

I'LL LOVE YOU,

LOVE YOU,

LOVE YOU,

EVERY, EVERY DAY.

Philip Blackburn is a professional speaker who serves as a keynote speaker, motivational specialist, and seminar leader for conventions and companies all over the country. For information about his speaking programs and children's books, or to order additional copies of *Every, Every Day* ($8.95 plus $1.00 postage and handling), write to:

Philip Blackburn
P.O. Box 8585
Orlando, FL 32856